Congr...

THE TEENAGE YEARS...
MAPPED.

Joshua Jamieson

jesperson publishing

2002 Jesperson Publishing

THE TEENAGE YEARS...
MAPPED.

JOSHUA JAMIESON
PHOTOGRAPHY: GILLIANE SITTMANN

100 Water Street
P. O. Box 2188
St. John's, NL
A1C 6E6

National Library of Canada Cataloguing in Publication Data

Jamieson, Joshua, 1984-
The teenage years... mapped / Joshua Jamieson

Poetry.
ISBN 1-894377-01-X
1. Adolescence--Poetry. I. Title.

PS8569.A4696T43 2002   C811'.6
C2002-905758-2   PR9199.4.J34T43 2002

photography: Gillianne Sittmann

cover and book design:

The Canada Council | Le Conseil des Arts
for the Arts | du Canada

We acknowledge the financial support of The Canadian Council
for the Arts for our publishing activities.

Printed in Canada.

Here it is,
finally in a book.
I decided to write it for you,
and now it is yours.

You can use it
to help you on your way
as you grow up,
as you reflect on life.

It will age with you,
some pages will be
rippled with tears
ripped with anger
and tattered with love.

This is yours,
and I hope it helps,
for this is your guide,
the teenage years,
mapped...

~

This book is dedicated to those of you whom
I have been blessed to have known and have
given me support.

Thanks mum for telling me that it is ok to write.

I also want to dedicate the book to anyone out
there who is struggling with any inner issue,
I promise you that it will get better, and you'll
have the courage someday.

~

@ the Forword

We're all born individuals, let's not die a copy.

It's funny you know, how something small, some tiny thought or short sentence can mean so much to someone. I read that phrase over two years ago, and I can honestly say, not a day goes by where I don't think about it. It really doesn't say that much in only nine words, basically portraying individuality above all else, at least that is how I look at it. Since the day that I read it I've taken it to heart, living everyday, striving to be me, or at least who I think I am. Much can be said for individuality and not becoming a sheep. Far too often we go and do something for the simple reason that - everyone else has. All too often we tell our children and youth certain teachings, almost preaching, to live life a certain way. This can often be confusing, and I am certainly not qualified to analyze the natures and tendencies of our society towards our next generation. In fact, I avoid analysis at most every opportunity, only dissecting something when absolute need exists. Why analyze when you can just enjoy? Sometimes something is exactly what it seems, granted that is not always the case.

So with that, take this book, this collection of a year and half of my writing, and read in to it what you will. It's the beauty of poetry, that you can become most intimate with it, personalizing every word with life experience or wish. Analyze it if you feel you must, be my guest.

Always remember though, to be yourself, embrace your individuality, never look back and have absolutely no regrets. Do things, and live your life the way you want to ... for you.

Where it's all @

A Place For The Misunderstood

Psycho

Freedom of expression.
I will do what I please,
so don't try to stop me.
Feel the artistry.
Watch me as I get high.
See my eyes glare,
roll up in my head.
Frustration in the fingers.
Pressure in the head.
Undersexed and over expressed.
Better off then before.
The world analyzes,
face value.
Maybe more maybe less.
The strange get attention,
so sink your teeth in.
Don't forget to hold on.
Now lets begin.

Circles

Change careers, plans, decisions
    crazed, looking for the one thing that few find.

          Spend hours thinking and dreaming
    thoughts coming and going over and over
like a broken record
        going around in circles.

            We search for love
      addicted to it.
Like rats in a maze
    will we ever get out of the maze?

Opening

I know life is hard sometimes,
every thing bottled up inside.
Our mind is the cage of our secrets.
We give only few the key.
Some choose to lose that key,
and friends keep and cherish it.

Those that lose it, or throw the key away,
are losing much more than just that key.
They have lost one of life's greatest gifts.

I've given some people my key,
most have kept it, I am very fortunate.
You've given me your key......
I'll keep it forever.

Displacement

You've left me here,
here all alone.

Who do you think you are?

You think you're big
.....and I am small.

Abandonment will only make me stronger.

Goliath fell
.....David didn't.

One Way Street

We are often suppressed, ignored, and underminded.
What do we know?
Don't you know that we're all out of control freaks ...
or so the assumption goes.

We are intelligent, and lead normal lives,
often stressful at times.
Just listen, be open, care.
Don't walk away.
Abandonment solves nothing.
Punishment only satisfy's the weak and shallow.
Suppression makes us stronger.

So many people that you choose to ignore for stupid
reasons.
You suppress us, you ignore our existence.
I think that you're the one who is the freak.
Tunnels only lead you to one place.

INVASION

What do you think you're doing?
You weak little thing you.
Waltzing in here and taking over.
Don't you even start.
Don't you even think you'll trample over me.
Just c'mon and try and we'll see who is left standing.
I wont beat you down with my physicallity.
I'll just win any way.
My mouth will do enough.
So don't think you're all that.
'Cause you're not nothing.
You're certainly something.
But you're nothing I want to be concerned with.
Get a life of your own.
Don't live through mine.
If I'm cold, I'm sorry.
But no one takes kindly,
to invasion.

When I'm famous ....

Why do you question me
on who I am?
And why I'm that way?
What difference does
it make?
Everyone tells me 'bout my
wrongs, my screw ups.
Well why don't you stop?
Just for a second, just stop.
Look at me and give a
compliment.
If you can't, then don't,
but just shut up.
I am who I am, because
I want to be that way.
Not because of you or
the guy next door.
I do what I want to
make me happy.
Someday I'll be rid. Rid
of you and this life.
I'll be famous. I'll forget
you when I'm famous.

Farewell, wave the white
hanky to the former me.
This is who I am. Take it
or leave it, 'cause I'm not
changing.
If you don't like it, that's
fine, its your loss, my dear.

I do what I want to make
me happy.

Someday I'll be rid. Rid of
you and this life.
I'll be famous. I'll forget
you when I'm famous.

You may think I'm a prick,
maybe a vindictive bitch,
or even egotistical. Well
if I'm a prick,
there must be something
to pop.
And if I'm a vindictive bitch,
then you gave me a reason.
And if you think I'm
egotistical,
well I say .. what's wrong
with ambition?

I do what I want to make
me happy
Someday I'll be rid. Rid of
you and this life.
I'll be famous.
I'll forget you when I'm
famous ... (prick)
I'll forget you when I'm
famous ... (bitch)
I'll forget you when I'm
famous ... (full of shit)
I'll forget you when I'm
famous....

Technicolor Love

Blind Kiss

The ridges, crevices, and bumps
of a finger allow touch.
Running my fingers across your forehead,
it's broad.
Then to the sides of your face,
dipping into where your eyes are,
you have beautiful eyes,
I know.
One hand graces your nose,
and the other on your cheek bone,
it's high.
A hand on your ear lobe,
as my finger falls from your nose,
onto the middle of your top lip.
My thumb runs across your lips,
and my other hand meets your chin,
and pulls your face.

1

You,
who is so pure
that I have gotten to know.
I am a hypocrite because I don't believe,
but love at first sight has occurred.
You,
that steals my sanity,
makes me feel at rest.
So I let you keep it.
My headstrong mind,
succumbs to your tempting attraction.
Now,
fortunate
that I am not condemned
to a life of wishing.
Dreams do come true.
The affliction of loneliness
has been abolished.
Thoughts of you have been
affirmed.
The night stretches her hand across
your face,
you smile,
you're beautiful,
you're sexy.
I am indignant for your embrace.
I long for your kiss.
You're all I think of.
All the world's a stage,
and you're the only one on it.
My star.
The keeper of my attention.
The one.

Epiphany

In life there are risks.
There are risks every day.
You do things,
take the risk,
whatever happens, happens.
And you wake up the next morning,
the same way that you always did, alive.
I felt different though,
mundane, no...
My heart was beating, and I was alive,
the difference... was that I was happy,
happy to be alive.
And you, you're the reason.
I don't know why,
but I don't question...
why you were brought
into my life.
Sure there have been others,
other guys, but you're not one.
You stand out, and I've given in.
After one kiss, you're with me
all the time.
All the time, I'm on cloud nine.
And it's you, it's because of you.
And I'm freed from the depths,
of a habitual day.
I still wake up every morning,
the same way that I always did, alive.
And I'm thankful to be alive.
But I'm privileged to have you.

Breathing A Moment

His porcelain lips
are glossy and shine in the sun.
They are tender,
and delicate.
So firm when they touch mine.
I can feel him inside.

His eyes are oceanic,
deep and moving with emotion.
They tell me the stories,
of his intellect and intimacy.
Speaking to my soul.

His hands, filled with warmth.
Touch my skin,
with empathy and feeling
for what is true and real.

I feel safe in his presence.

Free Falling

The way you make me feel
more then human
on a supernatural high.
You take me to a height
that no one else can,
where no one can reach me.
Lift me up and
enrapture my body
with your arms.
With eyes closed,
I can see all
that makes you whole,
and all your truth.
Your heart,
that is as young as tomorrow.
Your soul,
that is as pure as water.
Your mind,
that is as deep as a black hole.
Never let go of me,
for then I will surely fall
from this deadly height.

state

you are my life, the one that consumes me
i think about you and my stomach tingles
your image warms my heart
your face warms my soul
your smile is all my mind thinks of

people can give me the world
they can offer me everything
but all i want is a second with you
i want to share life with you

you are modest and do not see your beauty
but i do
i see your warmth which comes from within
and i see the truly pure person that you are

you make me feel like no other
i close my eyes
every muscle relaxes
in a state of quiescence

we reach out and our fingers touch
like men of the renaissance
men in Michelangelo's mind
fine art imprinted for a lifetime

we close our eyes
and our lips touch
in a state of depth
electrifying connection

The Dance

He lies next to me,
on the wooden patio,
getting drunk off the
rich night.
Turning to my side,
eyes closed.
My hand climbs
his side,
to rest on his
bare chest.
My chin rests on
his shoulder,
bodies shift,
his hip pushes in
to me.
He turns on to his side,
he gazes into,
the depths of my eyes.
His skin rests
expressionless,
on his face
staring at me.
Deep in thought.
Bodies become closer.
His hand runs through
my hair,
his teeth rub his
bottom lip.
We're thinking the
same thing.

The hand on my
head, falls to the
back of my neck.
Pulling my face to his,
we share a kiss.
His hand,
falls to the small
of my back,
he holds my body
against his.
Skin to skin.
The sense of touch
allows for
my escape.
His hand moves in
the back pocket
of my jeans.
He pulls me
closer again.
My hand still on
his chest,
upright, held
tightly between
two bodies.
My lips dance on his.
We fall asleep,
under the blanket
of stars.
Holding each other.

Catch 22

gotten used to your arms
and how you breathe
in to my ear when you lie next to me
your smile that I love
and coming home to your house
it's not really home for me
but it is the closest thing that I have for now
and I'll just have to be happy with that
and you're everything I need
tasting your lips is enough
nourishment for my body
strengthening me
giving me what I need
to keep on going
yeah keep on going
and making life work
but I hate it I hate it
for I'll only wilt and die
if your arms no longer hold me
my body will fall
weak to the floor
now I need you
to keep me alive
so now my love
don't leave
'cause you're sweet
and you're everything I need
and I am happy with that
just don't let me fall
catch me

Rookie

You can't understand
what it's like
until you've committed
the act.
You'll look at yourself
differently.
The mirror will reveal
your sheepish smile.
Content you will be,
and happy that you
did it, no regrets.
Even though tears may fall.

Family
Affair

Love With Prejudice

Maybe it's just stupid,
or even to the extreme of ridiculous.
In some ways such a waste,
but this fuel has kept me alive.
Pushed me to the edge of cliffs,
of tears, of discovery.
And I don't know why.
No I don't know why,
or even how.

I have achieved my own greatness,
made my own foundation, unbreakable.
Something you'll never change.
There is a part of me that hates you,
and the other part wishes for your eyes
to burn with tears.

At least look,
look for me, or try to care.
Then you tried ... at least.
It will never be enough,
and your touch still remains in my blood.

I am half you.
It is a curse to me,
and a blessing.

But I am all me in the end.

Breaking Out

I knew that there was that possibility there.
That from what I had heard it would never turn out...
How could it?
It always ruined lives,
I was mad and what the hell was I thinking.
Yeah, I didn't even know what was goin' through my
mind,
there were just too many things,
goin' too fast and I was in a spin.
But I had to do it,
because it was driving me mad,
I was ready for the nut house,
and they weren't ready for me.
I was new and what I was gunna do,
hadn't been done too often before.
It scared me, what could happen.
But I had trust and knowledge.
So I walked in,
in to the dim light,
young and trembling,
mouth opened wide,
but my tongue was dammed,
and the flow of words was stuck.

And as I stood there choking you held my hand.

Ying Yang

Humbled
in her life and in her grace.
She wouldn't approve,
of the lifestyle I've chosen,
but it is what makes me happy.
Things changed when she went,
I became more courageous.
It was because of her,
that the door was kept locked.
I can't say that I am happier now,
then I was then.
But now it is a different kind of happiness.
There are days that I miss her,
and when my friend went through the same thing,
the memories returned.
Truthfully I never really think of her everyday,
but as of late I have.
She was a truly wonderful woman,
one that should be remembered.
She had her quirks and perks,
like we all do.
And although she wouldn't approve of my life,
in ways,
it is because of her teachings that I am who I am.
She gave me the courage that allowed me to open
the door.
She kept me behind it,
but let me open it.

hidden

I'm stuck.
I'm fucked.
Something's taking over
and I can't handle it.

I've overcome feats
I've broken chains.
And now it's coming,
coming to ruin me.

Why, what is this?
What did I do to loose this?
It's my mind, my place.
My escape has been intruded.

You'll miss out
because I'm hidden
in a shadow that's so small.
But you've been blinded.

So I guess I'm just outta luck.
I guess I'll just have to deal.
I guess I'm fucked.

Worth Seeing

I see the way you run
into his arms,
your face filled with 1000
words.
Words you can't even say.

I see the way you fall
in to her chest,
so quickly you've attached
to what's mine.
What I willingly share.

I see the ways you
turn your head,
with a smile.
Vogue child, vogue.

I see the way you've
opened my eyes.
You've opened them to
empathy and experience.
Young Life,
I see you.
Never change,
express emotions,
hold on to heritage,
live life.
Be you,
because,
that is what is worth seeing.

–
Washed Out
in
Black
and
White
_

Shattered Crystal

God it was sweet,
the way it worked.
What once was perfect,
had reoccurred.

I thought it was over,
done forever.
There would never be
another day we'd spend
together.
But I was wrong,
and you once again came
along.
Wowed my heart.
Soothed my soul.
Wooed me all over again.

And all over again,
just when I thought ...
You found a new way
to break my heart.

Moving On

Do you understand,
what it feels like,
and how to deal with it?

Can you grasp the fact,
that I find it hard
to see you now?

'Cause what you've done,
to me was uncalled for,
and inhuman.

I once held you tight
and it felt so good,
it was so right.

But what's done is done
and it's over now.
I want to love you,
but I just wouldn't know how.

'Cause now that you're gone
I just feel so much better now
and I know that it won't take long
there are other men and I'll love again.

Sting

I liked you
and your ways.
About life,
and how you lived.
Carefree and
you always had what you wanted.

You wanted it
so you asked.
When that wasn't enough,
you demanded.
When that wasn't enough,
you forced.

I liked you till then,
until I found out what you were.
The cold stone that is your heart,
the unlit darkness that is your soul.

I even got over that,
kept my fingers in touch.
In my placid life,
you remained.
Until you made your demands again.
When you became forceful again.

Get out, just leave.
I knew you were wrong for me,
when I kissed your mouth.
Your sharp tongue,
cut me inside,
and the words you left,
sting like salt.

The Great Search

It was great,
he loved you so,
the one that you thought was right.
You're only young though,
and you know that you won't find
Mister Man over night.
Keep your chin hunny,
or let the tears roll,
be strong or be weak,
it's ok with me.
My arms are here to hold you up,
and my shoulder is here for your head.
I know it's tough,
and it's hard to see him go,
it's hard to let go of.
When you think you're in love,
it doesn't matter if you really are.
Just remember that life is learning,
and he'll just have to be another stamp
in your passport.
You've got your memories,
recall them if you like,
and just keep on going.
I promise you that someday,
you'll find mister right.

All It Takes

He said
she said
that they went and did that
and then I heard,
you tell,
that guy,
that it was so good.
So what's the story?
Where is the accountability?
You told me that you didn't.
But did you?
What you told me,
was it really true?
Or did you just want to fuck me over too?
See when I heard,
them say,
over there,
that you really did,
I didn't think so,
I thought it was a no go,
they were so wrong.
I defended you.
You told me otherwise,
and I believed you.
What am I to believe now?
Walk your way out,
make sure you don't falter,
you're stories are beginning to crumble.
I'll always be there...
You don't really care...
Just you go and get laid...
Really I don't mind...
It wont be my fault when the lights start to fade...

Ripple Effect

There you go again,
harping on the past,
how hard it was.
But happy you are,
telling the stories
over and over again
about how shallow it was,
and how vain he is.
My ears listened every time.
My lips never complained.
My senses took to your needs,
and empathy for you
took over my thoughts.
We drove by today,
after you didn't answer the phone.
It was strange to me.
My eyes burned in the reflection of the glass.
"Apartment for rent".
Where were you
and where was the empathy for me?
Still waters run deep,
and you just moved.

Addiction

It is a drug ...
I need it ...
I want it.
Yearning for my next fix.
Hours spent on the high.
Care free.
Happiness and bliss.
Nothing else matters.
A new day.
A new fix.
This new drug,
it is so cheep.
I want it every night.
I get it every night .....
But only for a few months.
Then the supply ends,
it is over.
I am lost.
I don't know what to do.
Weak.
Vulnerable.
I break down.
Crying.
Collapsed on the floor.
I have lost a piece of me,
a piece of my life.
I miss him.

Sinking

Lying on the floor,
looking at the ceiling.
Eyes open but deep,
in thought.
Swollen lips,
pressed together.
Arms crossed on the
surface of a chest.
Legs spread apart,
feet pointing to the sky.
Body is lifeless.
Mind is pensive,
on thought.
Music plays from a stereo.
Notes trigger thoughts,
and emotions.
A single tear emerges,
beads on the cheek,
gravity pulls it to the carpet,
leaving a glistening,
wet trail.
The chimes are thrown,
carelessly about,
and the last chord cries,
from the piano,
and sinks into silence.
The body feels like
it's sinking into the floor,
the mind wishes it was
sinking into your arms.

Tidal

your love comes over me
like a tidal wave
it washes over my body
I do not drown

love grows
like plant life
it takes time to mature
but it will

love continues
like a bird wings outstretched
flying
in the open sky
with no real destination
just destiny guiding

you profess your love
to me
writing it in the sand.
a tidal wave washes
over

–
Mind
your
imagination
–

Faith

He is my creator
the one that
holds the threads
and the scissors
I have my faith
he has my thread
what he chooses to do
he will do
I refuse to fall to my knees
he knows I exist
and I know he exists
I don't need physicality
and alters and shrines
and makeshift illusions
and rules
I don't need to be in a cult
I have
faith
in me
and in him

Three Dimensional Darkness

Have you ever sat in the dark?
Come home from work,
let your coat fall to the floor,
undone the top button in your jeans,
and somehow between the door and
the couch your socks managed to scuff off.
Then you stand at the foot of
the couch and fall backwards,
trusting the couch to be there.
But instead you wish that it was the arms
of your lover.

Have you ever been left in the dark?
Been told two contradictory things, from the same lips?
Only the time spent in between hearing, was spent loving.
And now it's not the same,
and it never will be again.

Have you ever been alone in the dark?
Lying on the floor with your arms crossed
and placed behind your head, so that your head
is propped up and you can look around.
Your eyes wide open, still blinded
until a car drives by the naked window
and a square of light takes over the wall.

Have you ever been with someone in the dark?
Someone that you love, that you can cuddle into.
Someone that you're willing to do anything for.
Both pairs of eyes are closed as you waltz holding each other.

The dark allows dreams.
The dark is cold.
The dark is lonely.
The dark is relaxing.
What will you think when you turn out the light tonight?

irreconcilable differences

love is the worst
feeling in the world
unloved is what
no one wants
to be loved
is all that is coveted
but it is brutal
leaving you smashed
unrepairable
what a waste
it is
to try to love
and
what a waste
it is
to be
unloved
leaving you
lost
drop and fall
into confusion
or bliss
close your eyes
and dream

Lust

Her body lies,
across the burgundy satin.
Dim lights grace her face,
and her clothes have been strewn
across the room.
Her chin, so slender and shaped
is facing up,
allowing her neck to lie vulnerable,
showing her grace as would a crane.
Her face shows great satisfaction
and pleasure, her eyes are closed,
and her lips are lightly pressed
with her lipstick removed by a neck.
Her arm is outstretched and her hand
is open slightly with her fingers disarrayed.
Her head flinches and turns to the wall
as a tear falls and the door slams.
She has been used.
He has hurt her,
and broken her heart.
Passion has been stolen,
love has been lost,
in this night of lust.

Cold Air

Standing by the road the other day,
Looking up at the way it curved.
Hearing in my mind the screams and shock,
that gushed from the mouth.

Better then blood,
or was it really?
It almost feels worse...

Unfledged children were affected.
Such a sin that unripened lives
have been slowed to a crawl,
by the epitome of judgement.

Mortality is realized.
Helplessness is evident.
Life is wilting, wilted.

My Space

The weight of the sound
in the room was nothing.
Warm soft yellowish light
cast shadows through this place.
Creating a like image of reality
in silhouette on the painted wall.
With a mind so overwrought with thought,
the eyes stare into the space, blankly.
Mouth gaping open.
Sometimes it's nice to get lost,
please don't find me.

Address Book

By the time you hit twenty,
how many hands have you shaken?
How many names have you heard?
And how many people have you met?
No one has really counted,
but if you ask,
the list will reach arms lengths.
Even though not every name,
encounter, moment, and person will be included,
a lot of them will be.
The ones that are usually included are usually
included for a reason.
It could be because they did something amazing,
or maybe they can do something for you.
But there are some people that are just included,
and we can't really put a finger on a reason.
There has to be a reason though.
It can probably be attributed
to some type of greatness.
My guess is that greatness is time.
Time which has been invested.
Time which has been spent teaching.
In this life, we're all teachers.
And time should be spent thanking those teachers.

Void

A world without dance,
no laughter,
and laboured conversation.
Destitute for thought.
Choking on life.
It could be worse.
Unstoppable.
But hopeful regret,
is wished upon.
Untravelled roads,
need guidance,
and a clenched hand.
A reckless dream
left bruised reality.
Reality will heal,
but minds are scarred.

Slap In The Face

The bleak horizon that I saw
when I looked out my window today.
It put me in a mood,
one where I wanted to stay home.
Just stay home in my bed and not move.
I knew that something would happen that day.
So I dragged out of bed,
forced my eyes to feed on the light.
The horizon was bleak and void
but it still hurt my eyes.
The thought of making it
through the day ahead
was a frustration.
The frustration was there,
I couldn't solve all the dilemmas,
and I couldn't control my life entirely.
I was losing control of everything,
and was afraid of not being able to find it again.
I think we're all that way,
just a little bit is all we need.
Enough to delude reality
because a lot of the time,
reality sucks.

Second After

Enchanting
is the touch
that I have
experienced.
Feelings
and emotions
running wild,
fast, and furious.
Left in a whirl,
never-ending,
spinning.
Isn't it amazing?
You just don't
realize what
it is like.
Looking down,
there is your body,
it isn't a dream!
Mouth gaped
open and head
cocked back.
Sigh and the
comatose
continues.

Sensory Overload

Hey there you,
yeah you
you know you want it.
So how are you gunna get it?
You can reach and grab,
get physical, make skin touch.
But don't be brassy,
don't be bold.
You be good, and do as you're told.
We don't need to be rough,
use your word, it can be tough.

Hey there you,
yeah you,
come ... c'mon, come here.
Follow me and let it go.
Don't hold on for the ride.
Live it.
Feel it.
Let it go and relax.
Lean back and enjoy the show,
it's got rave reviews.
Don't be frightened, you can do anything here.
Act your own part.
Cry with joy,
sweat with anticipation,
or open your mouth and scream.
I'll be with you, I'll guide you.
It'll be fun in the end,
so listen to me.
'Cause you know you want to,
come with me
on sensory overload.

Murder

It rests,
covered with the
blood
of the innocent.
All shamelessly killed.
By a killer,
who has no regrets,
no remorse,
no feelings,
no cares.
Mother nature
graces the bloodshed
with her fingertips.
Rain.
The windshield,
the killer,
washes clean
and there are
a few less bugs in the world.

Joshua Jamieson was born, Joshua Donald Patrick Jamieson in St. John's, Newfoundland and Labrador on June 11, 1984. He is presently a first year student at Memorial University completing a Bachelor of Arts with a double major in English and Political Science.

Josh has been active in the business community since the age of eight when he had a Worm Stand in front of his uncles store. That was followed by three years of selling Regal and the establishment of a web design business in 1998, Perfect Pages Web Design, from which he branched out into marketing and desktop publishing. Jamieson has freelanced as a youth reporter for the CBC for three years and presently co-hosts a radio show for youth, Fresh Focus, on Radio Newfoundland.

Josh has always had an interest in the written word, being an avid reader as a child. This interest, coupled with his sense of community led him to produce a play; "All I Really Need to Know, I Learned in Kindergarten" at the age of 16 with partial proceeds going to charity. The play was later produced for the Avalon East School Board Drama Festival making history by being the first play to be split between three high schools as a joint production. Josh's sense of community continues as he serves on a Provincial Youth political Association as well as several community interest groups.

Since 1999 Jamieson has been active with global Vision and Junior Team Canada, a Graduate of the Economic Training Center in 1999, a Leader as well as the Atlantic Representative on the Junior Team Canada Trade Mission to Germany and Austria in 2000, and the Regional Coordinator of the program for 2001 and 2002.

Josh first began writing in High School as a way of coping with the day-to-day stresses of teenage life and soon discovered that it was something that he enjoyed. He is currently working on a second book of poetry as well as his first novel.